AF589359

No 2

The Deep Meadow
Meditations for children
The Mild Winds
Meditations for children
The Flamedancers' Fire
Meditations for children
BEDTIME STORIES
Let sleep come easily with this FIRE meditation. Create a deep connection with your child and help them to recharge.
Gitte Winter Graugaard
Meet Chief Eaglefeather
Meditations for children
Gitte Winter Graugaard

THIS IS BOOK TWO IN THE SERIES **THE VALLEY OF HEARTS**

An amazing series of books with child meditations written by Gitte Winter Graugaard. Show your child how to reach their inner valley. "Meet Chief Eaglefeather" (no 1) and let him teach you to use the four elements: Fire, Water, Earth, and Air. Help your child cleanse their own energy with "The Flamedancers' Fire" (no 2). Cleanse off other people's energies under "The Clear Cascade" (no 3). Find peace in "The Deep Meadow" (no 4). Fly high to get new perspective on "The Mild Winds" (no 5).

www.thevalleyofhearts.com

#kidsmeditate

To

____

____

Your personal note to the child you give this book to

____

____

____

____

From

____

____

The Flamedancers' Fire

Meditations for children

By Gitte Winter Graugaard

Illustrations by

Elsie Ralston

Room for Reflection Publishing

"We all wish to see the spark in our children's smiling eyes, and we dream that they will fall in love with life itself and explore the many adventures life has to offer, and feel connected. One way to make this happen is to teach our children about their inner fire - their passion power - and how to tend to it.

Helping your child to balance their inner fire is helping them to navigate their future. It is a gift for life".

- Gitte Winter Graugaard

The books in the series The Valley of Hearts are:

- Meet Chief Eaglefeather
- The Flamedancers' Fire
- The Clear Cascade
- The Deep Meadow
- The Mild Winds

Other books published in English:

- The Children's Meditations In my Heart
- Heartlight - teach your child to shine

The series will be available in several languages in the future.

See where we're at with our words here: www.gittewintergraugaard.dk

♡ ♡ ♡

My dear reader

I am so excited for you. You have made your way to The Valley of Hearts and now get to know about the magical Flamedancers' Fire.

Let's light up our children and empower them to fall in love with life and shine even brighter.

Much love
Gitte Winter Graugaard

www.thevalleyofhearts.com

The Flamedancers' Fire, Meditations for Children
A book from the series The Valley of Hearts

1st edition in English 2021

Author: Gitte Winter Graugaard
Illustrations: Elsie Ralston
Layout: Katrine Høyer
Translation: Eva Juul, Gitte Winter Graugaard
Editor: Sam Jennings

ISBN: 978-87-93210-34-9 (paperback)
ISBN: 978-87-93210-58-5 (hardbound)
ISBN: 978-87-93210-36-3 (e-book)
ISBN: 978-87-93210-35-6 (PDF)

Room for Reflection Publishing

♡♡♡

Table of contents

♡♡♡

Let me introduce you to
The Flamedancers' Fire

Introduction to The Flamedancers' Fire

What would happen if all children and parents were taught to tend to their inner fire? How would that transform family energies all over the world? Those were the questions I asked myself when I began writing this meditation. Hearing from many parents in Denmark how helpful this training has proven to their family unit as a whole, I decided to share it with the rest of the world.

This book can be read to children from the age of 5, depending on the maturity of the child, and older children into their teens.

Welcome to this second book in The Valley of Hearts series. In the first book, I introduced you to the valley, and talked you through how to "get there". On arrival in the valley you met our guide, the wise Chief Eaglefeather. I recommend you begin by reading the first book however you can still use this book independently.

In this second book, Chief Eaglefeather takes you and your child to visit the magical Flamedancers' Fire. Are you excited to learn more about your inner fire and help your child find balance with this life-giving element?

This meditation is helpful for both parents and children who have either too much inner fire or too little. It also helps those of you who already have your fire element in balance, maintain this balance and become more conscious of the importance of keeping your inner fire in check.

The meditation presented in this book is a guided visualization that you and your child co-create together with Chief Eaglefeather and the element of fire. As your child is guided into the meditation with closed eyes, they will be able to delve deeper into the sceneries and energies of the book. And by the use of their breathing, senses and imagination, your child can find all the magic that resides inside of them. Recently I visited a school in Nottingham, in England, to teach the students heart meditation. Each time I asked a class of pupils in grade 3: "Why do you think I love working with children? Why are children so special compared to adults when it comes to meditation?" one of the first replies was: "We have a better imagination". I really believe this to be true, so encourage your child to open up to their imagination. And observe your child and see if you can let go of your perhaps analytical mind and drift with your child into a more imaginative world.

A gift for life

Our inner fire is crucial to us for so many reasons. While reading this book I invite you to zoom in on your own inner fire as a parent, teacher or caregiver around children, and try to become more conscious of your own fire, and then the fire of your child or children if you are teaching a group. There is so much to investigate when it comes to inner fire and so much to learn.

We all want our children to grow up full of passion and joy, have healthy relationships with friends and family, one day find the love of their lives, grow a wonderful family out of love, and pursue a career they are really passionate about. We wish to see that spark in their eyes, and we dream that they will fall in love with life itself and explore the many adventures life has to offer, and feel connected. One way to make this happen is to teach our children about their inner fire - their passion power - and how to tend to it. Helping your child to balance their inner fire is helping them to navigate their future. It is a gift for life.

When we teach energy cleansing methods to our children, we equip them with tools to self-regulate, which they can use throughout the day whilst at school. That will likely mean they will get into fewer arguments. And if they do pick a fight, they might feel it is easier to move on afterwards. It is very likely that it will become easier for them to fall asleep at night as they will let go of what potentially weighs on them. They might even sleep longer and deeper as well.

Out of balance

When you walk into a schoolyard or a kindergarten today, you will quickly see that not all children have balance in their inner fire, and for many reasons. At one end of the spectrum we see the 'invisible' children, children who have been taught to dim their light, hide their emotions and not make a fuss. At the other end we see highly tempered children, who hit, scream, kick or get very upset. I am not sure which group feels the worst. Neither is happy; neither is in a state of balance. It is our job to help them navigate through life and find balance.

Where on the scale below would you place yourself and your child?

Invisible	Anonymous	In balance	Tempered	Near explosion

The art of letting go

Tending to their inner fire will help invisible and anonymous children turn up their fire, enabling them to experience a more balanced energy.

It will also help tempered and explosive children dial down their inner fire, enabling them to find a more peaceful balance and better ways to communicate. As with all things in life, it is all about finding that inner balance where joy can sparkle and love can flourish.

With this fire meditation, I help you teach your child to sift through the many inputs of the day and to recognize which have made an impression, and how they feel about them. You learn how to let go of pent-up energy from thoughts, feelings and experiences you no longer want to carry. When you throw the excess energy that burdens you onto the fire, you will most likely feel lighter.

Getting to know your inner fire

Before reading the meditation, I encourage you to first reflect upon the meaning of fire in your life. Take some time to reflect and maybe take some notes. By becoming more conscious of your inner fire while working with the wisdom of this book and that of nature, you might look back at your notes and realize how much you have learned from zooming in on your fire – often within a short period of time.

Many parents sit back with a feeling of remembering old wisdom long forgotten when they begin working with the elements. I sure did. Our children are great teachers too. They often come with a deep understanding of the elements around and inside of us, and they simply pay better attention as they are in a state of learning. Use the beginner's mind of your child to experience the world again. Try asking yourself the following:

- What is your relationship with fire?
- When do you light fire?
- Do you use fire in your daily routine? Yes? No? Sometimes?
- Do you think about your inner fire?
- Are you grateful for the fire in your daily routine? Or do you barely recognize it?
- Are you joyful? Do you consider yourself a passionate person? Do you show true commitment in your work?
- Do you connect your passion to your inner fire, and if yes how?
- Would you say you have a lot of fire, or only a little?
- Try to picture your inner fire and the shape of it. Maybe try to draw it together with your child. What would your inner fire look like?
- Do you feel the fire within your body? If so, how and where?
- Are you more inclined to feel hot rather than cold, or the other way around?

- What are the main characteristics of fire to you?
- Pay attention to your findings above - are they positive or negative in character?
- Do you recognize many or few of these characteristics of fire within yourself?
- Are you hot-tempered or rather a slow burner?
- Do you sometimes feel under fire? When?
- Do you sometimes feel burned out? When?
- Do you have a short fuse or a long one? How does it show?
- Do you feel ignited or rather extinguished? Do you know why?
- Do you mostly resemble a small steady flame, a roaring fire or the last embers of the ashes?

With these questions, you can already see how much our daily language and expressions are influenced by the energy of the element fire.

You will most likely begin to hear more expressions in your language that indicate how powerful the elements are to the human mind. I love finding all these little indicators of the importance of the elements in our daily lives.

To me language serves as a reminder of the relevance of the elements and the history of their importance in our lives. It almost feels like a treasure hunt of sorts. Just follow the little signs and pay attention!

Zoom in on your child's inner fire

Now contemplate the same questions above but focus instead on how they relate to your child. Consider whether your child shows interest in the element of fire. Maybe there are clues as to whether they manifest a lack of interest, normal interest or great interest therein. Does your child seek fire? Does your child love to help start a camp fire, roast marshmallows, light candles, light the fireplace and such things? Or perhaps your child is afraid of fire?

If your child is older, you can discuss the questions below. Otherwise, think about the questions and take notes. This exercise and the observations made can be very revealing for parents. And your notes or the notes your child makes here can become very valuable to your child later in life.

How do you perceive the characteristics of fire in your child?

What is your child's relationship to fire?

Is your child passionate? Does your child show true commitment?

Would you say your child has a lot of fire, or only a little?

How do you think your child feels fire within themselves?

How does your child talk about fire in general? Is your child attracted to fire or more resentful of it?

Do you recognize many or few of the characteristics of fire within your child?

Is your child hot-tempered or a slow burner?

Can you feel your child's passion? Do you know what gets your child fired up?

Does your child sometimes feel under fire? Or do they more often feel burned out?

Does your child have a short or a long fuse?

Is your child lit, ablaze or rather extinguished?

Does your child mostly resemble a small steady flame, a roaring fire or the last embers of the ashes?

Other things to add?

Depending on the age of your child I encourage you to put some of these questions to your child and maybe have your child draw their inner fire on the next pages.

Ask how it feels

You can also ask them to show you where in the body they feel their inner fire. Ask them to draw the shape of the feeling of fire and colour it. Ask questions and pay attention. You can use the drawing below. You can also use the black and white fire element in the back of the book for your child to colour.

Working with a group of children

If you work with more children try looking at them individually and explore whether you can recognize the characteristics of fire within each child.

Try exploring both the tuning into fire in its natural form and the characteristics of fire, such as being able to flare up or almost burn out. Perhaps these initial observations and reflections can give you an idea of which children in your group are "fiery" and which are "dimmed", and as you read, let the meditation give you ideas as to how you might help them.

Fire in balance: Which children are passionate and dedicated in your group of children? Who lights up the whole room? Who is in balance?

Too little fire: Who seems more extinguished? Which children are more invisible and anonymous? Who is uncertain about themselves and their wishes? Who will benefit from turning up their fire?

Too much fire: Who is hot-tempered? Who easily erupts? Turns red? Spins out of control? Who could benefit from turning down their inner fire?

Try to look behind these characteristics in the children. Maybe you can detect why they are or aren't in balance? Maybe you know their parents, their circumstances or can see triggers within their environment.

Maybe you already recognize charateristics of each of the children you work with. You can make your notes on the next page.

Invisible

Anonymous

In balance

Tempered

Near explosion

Lift your vibration with fire

When presenting *The Flamedancers' Fire* to children, we give them a powerful tool to help cleanse their minds, both when they have too much and too little fire. In the world of meditation and inner work, fire has multiple effects: one effect you might already know comes from the calm we often feel when looking into the embers and flames of a fire. Tapping into this feeling of calmness by connecting to fire is helpful all day long, and can especially help around bedtime when children cleanse their energy and sift through the inputs of the day.

A fire can help us clear our minds whether we sit by a fire physically or in meditation. The flames can take away accumulated energy from emotions, thoughts and events that have settled in our minds, and bring us down into a lower vibration.

When we look at energy, we seek to hold a high vibration. And when we feel heavy, burdened, burned out and exhausted, these are all signs of a low vibration. With meditation and connection to nature we can change our frequency.

So many things often change when we lift our vibration. We attract people and projects at the same frequency we hold ourselves. So, helping our children maintain a high frequency and know how to cleanse and raise their vibration is incredibly powerful. I like to think of it as like helping an old record player that is stuck in a loop, playing the same tune. By lifting up the stylus and placing it in a better loop, we can choose a better track for us. That is what meditation often does for me.

If this sort of heavy influence in our energy isn't taken care of on a regular basis, over time it might take up so much space that it will most likely be noticed in our mood, our wellbeing, maybe even in our health. When your child learns to throw burdening excess energy onto the fire using this meditation, it is like clearing their mind and enabling them to shift their focus onto something that nurtures them instead, such as self-love.

A third gain from working with fire is learning to tune into our passion. This might be one of life's most important lessons. Learning to tap into our love and living a passionate life is the goal for most people, and yet so many of us find this hard to do. So hard in fact, that the WHO is predicting stress and depression to be the biggest diseases worldwide by 2030.

Let's get better at tending to our inner fires as parents so that we don't burn out, and let's teach the next generation how to tend to their inner fire and how to find passion.

Good to know before we begin

How to read the books

Tips and Tricks

Before we begin I will share with you a few tips that will enable you to get the best experiences with this book.

Always let your child find peace before embarking on the adventure into the valley.

In the first book you get a longer introduction on how to arrive in The Valley by helping your child breathe deeply into their belly. You can read from the first book, or use the shorter introduction I have included here in this book.

With my own children, I found that as we had already practised our *Arrival into the valley* for some time, I was able to shorten the introduction and spend more time on the actual releasing of energy and balancing of the element.

Use your intuition to guide you in this regard with your child. Children often love repetition. So maybe your child will want to hear the introduction more times than you. Be patient and trust that your child knows what they need. Also, shorten the meditation if you feel it is too long or add to it if that would make sense for you.

Look at this meditation as a starting point, a framework, and let your intuition guide you into making the right meditation for your child. Use longer pauses, replace words, skip parts, go more in depth - adapt according to what you sense is to your child's liking.

Keep calm

Pay attention to your own energy. It is crucial for your child's experience with meditation that you stay calm. Take your time and if you feel stressed before you begin, breathe deep down into your stomach. Let your child see how you use your own breath to calm yourself, and talk about how it works. You doing your inner work is the best way to teach them. Focus on your love for your child as you breathe and begin to connect with your love.

You being calm and present is key to making this work.

It is very normal that children move around during meditation as they begin to feel their bodies. One of my daughters swirls around ten times before she gets calm, the other one barely moves. There is no right or wrong here.

If your child talks during the meditation, you can calmly say: "Try to listen to this meditation and open up to your imagination. I am sure you can do this. Tomorrow or later you can tell me what you experience. But for now, it is time to be quiet and just enjoy the meditation."

Accept the noise around you, if there is any. We can't stop the turmoil of the world, but we can learn how to navigate it. Take an extra deep breath if you get annoyed at your child or lose focus. It will trigger your inner fire to ignite if you get annoyed or become angry with your child. Your child will likely mirror this emotion - get upset, ignite their inner fire - which isn't helpful when we try to balance this element.

Breathe through it.

Signs and signals

Whilst reading, you will see three hearts:

They signal time to pause your reading and give your child time to contemplate. You will find that we read these meditations at a slower pace and more calmly than regular bedtime stories.

You might naturally speak in a softer, deeper tone and use your breath to stay calm yourself. Often a little yawn in the beginning will make my children yawn as well, which facilitates deeper breathing.

When you encounter areas of text in italics or (brackets) mid-page in the meditation, it is a small message offering you alternatives or help.

You will also be encouraged to make your child the main character of the meditation, by mentioning the child's name whenever you find an open, underlined space in the text ______________. Feel free to mention your child by name more often if you sense that it inspires them. If you read to more children address them in the plural.

Different endings

If your child is familiar with my other book *The Children's Meditations In My Heart*, you can easily end the fire meditation by letting your child fill his or her heart with love. We do this all the time at home. First, we cleanse and balance using one of the elements, and then the children fall asleep while filling their hearts with love.

In this meditation we teach our children to get rid of negative energy and we then replace the space of that energy with self-love and compassion. Think about our bodies as a tank of energy. As you cleanse and empty out the tank there will be space to fill it up with something you really like. You can use the gateway I have written at the end of the meditation to move into the love mountain.

It will be easier for your child if you yourself are familiar with this book beforehand. So please go ahead and read it to yourself first, and maybe begin to reflect upon your inner fire.

Reading to a group

When I teach meditation in groups I find that some lay down immediately, some move about, and some have a very hard time engaging. It often turns out that those who have the hardest time engaging in the meditation need meditation the most. So please be patient.

If you read the meditation in your class and some pupils begin to yawn, it is a good signal. Encourage them to keep on yawning. In a class setting it can be a signal of impoliteness related to boredom to yawn, so some pupils will find it embarrassing. In meditation yawning is a good thing. Also, small bodily noises can occur from the stomach as we shift from the sympathetic nervous system to the parasympathetic nervous system. Again, you can help your pupils by saying it is very normal that our body expresses the joy of a break by sending small sounds as we begin to relax.

If more pupils sit next to each other and make fun of the meditation, I often move over and sit down in between them. If I know the children I will softly place a hand on them to help them relax and feel their body. I will also try to share my deep-rooted energy with them to help them relax.

I never force children to take part in meditation, but I will ask them to be quiet to not disturb their friends, who might need the meditation.

Some children don't want to close their eyes. It is a sign of unease or even fear, and should not be forced. Instead I tell them to fix their eyes on one spot in the room. When I come into a classroom, I can analyze the level of comfort and safety in the class by how many will close their eyes. If all pupils close their eyes, I can tell they have a good classroom environment and teachers who make them feel safe. This is however, not always the case. And for some children they carry fear into the classroom from their home environment. Meditating in class will help these children find the peace at school that they might not have access to at home.

Five steps to a better experience with child meditation:

1. Make sure you are calm before you start reading.

2. Keep calm while reading and pay attention to your energy.

3. Read slowly and pause during the reading.

4. Give the children time to open up to their imagination, contemplate, drift into the meditation and explore their inner world. In the days after, have the child draw what they have seen and be curious about what they draw.

5. Use your intuition to change words, the length of the meditation or include meanings that will help your child. Trust that you know what the child needs. Feel that you are being guided.

Enjoy this special time with your child. It could become one of those golden moments you can hold in your heart forever. Child meditation at bedtime has given me so many of those moments with my children.

Let's meditate

The Flamedancers' Fire

Meditation: The Flamedancers' Fire

Dear____________________ (insert NAME or "Children" if you have more listeners).

Deep down in the tummies of all children we can find a very special place called The Valley of Hearts. You get there by taking deep breaths. Come, let's try it together. Let's try to reach the valley and go on an inner adventure together. Let's go meet our friend Chief Eaglefeather and see what magic he has ready for us today.

You have so much power inside of you and I love when you find it. Because once you know just how beautiful, magical, and strong you are inside, life becomes both easier and more fun.

When you are ready, lie or sit down comfortably. Settle and cover up with a blanket if you like. Make yourself comfortable. Feel the ground underneath you. Connect to the ground.

Focus your attention on your breathing.

Breathe in through your nose, and out through your mouth.

Calmly.

♡♡♡

Find your inner peace. This special moment is all yours. Right here and right now, you don't have to perform, to pretend, or to look a particular way. In The Valley of Hearts you are welcome - just the way you are.

♡♡♡

Close your eyes when you are ready.

(If your child won't close their eyes, try saying the following: "If you aren't ready to close your eyes yet, please find a spot on the ceiling or on the wall upon which to focus. Once you feel ready, you can close your eyes.")

Finding inner peace by breathing deeply gives you access to The Valley of Hearts. In a short while, when you are completely calm, maybe with your eyes closed, and your body completely relaxed, you will find your way.

Maybe a little yawn will get your there.

Now imagine that you arrive in The Valley of Hearts.

Imagine that you are standing in a splendid meadow surrounded by the most magnificent mountains. It is the most wonderful summer day. In the beautiful blue sky above, the summer sun is hanging high, ready to warm your lovely body. A slight breeze bids you welcome. See if you can feel the breeze on your skin. Maybe you can feel the warm sun caressing your skin. It is one of those summery days you love the most.

Tune into your ears and listen.

Right in front of you a striking river is flowing by. Can you hear the rippling? The river is happy to see you; chuckling, it welcomes you to the valley. The whole valley is so happy that you decided to come for a visit. The trees, the mountains, the river, the birds love to see you.

Tune into your nose.

Can you smell the fresh water from the river?

Can you smell the freshness of the meadow?

Can you smell the scent of summer?

On the opposite side of the river, you notice a camp with a group of tepee tents. As you explore the camp, you soon notice a very special man on a small rock by the riverside. He stands tall and proud, with one foot in front of the other. His muscles are distinct and his cheekbones pronounced. As he sees you, his face lights up and you feel drawn towards him.

Here is Chief Eaglefeather waiting for you. Swiftly, he jumps down from the rock, and walks cheerfully towards you and breaks into a wide smile.

"There you are! I have been waiting for you. I am so happy to see you. I was so hoping you would come and visit me today. I have something very special to show you. Come along, my friend," he says and pulls out his hand towards you. As you grab it, he gives your hand a little, loving squeeze.

"________ Name______________________ today, we're visiting The Flamedancers' Fire," Chief Eaglefeather says, and points towards the biggest fire in the camp.

"Can you see the smoke over there? Yes, right over there.
Maybe you can smell the smoke? The white smoke rising to the skies from the large fire is something very special. Now let's go to the fire, so you can get to know it and experience the magic of it."

You look around you as you walk through the camp to the fire with Chief Eaglefeather.

As you come near you see other children and adults already sitting around the fire. "Here, at the fire, there is room for everyone. We welcome you no matter who you are, how you look or where you come from. Around the fire we are all the same. The fire only sees our souls. You are loved for being you. Just like we love the variety of our meadow for being so full of different flowers in all colours and shapes, so are the little differences in children loved and cherished here in the valley. Each child is a flower. All flowers are special, and together we make the most stunning bouquet," Chief Eaglefeather says.

From the energy around the fire, you can feel that everyone is feeling well and safe, and that they like sitting here undisturbed, each in their own little world without interruption from one another.

The experiences we have at this magic fire are each our own. There is nothing right or wrong. Your experience is yours to keep or share as you please.

♡♡♡

Chief Eaglefeather shows you where to sit on a beautiful fur; blankets are ready waiting to make you comfortable. The fur is soft and feels nice on your skin as you sit down.

♡♡♡

"Let me tell you about the magic of the fire and the element of fire," Chief Eaglefeather says, and sits down next to you. "Every day my friends in the valley and I visit this fire together with all the children who come to see us during the day, and especially at bedtime. The fire is an important tool for us, when we want to feel good inside; it also helps us to achieve all of our dreams.

You see, we all carry an inner fire. Knowing how to tend to our inner fire is such a gift. For some that comes easly, for others they find it difficult to tame their inner fire.Sometimes the fire can become so fierce, it feels like there is a volcano inside us, spewing fire, making us furious. That isn't comfortable, not for us nor for the people we are with. It overwhelms us and our surroundings. If that also happens to you, you can ask the fire to help you turn down your inner fire and find more balance," says Chief Eaglefeather, and asks you to think about your inner fire. Do you ever feel like a volcano about to explode? If yes, how does that feel?

"Other people have a different relationship with fire. To them, it can feel like the fire inside has been extinguished and has disappeared entirely. In that case, it can be difficult to feel yourself and choose what you would like to do. You can feel dimmed or almost empty inside. Do you know that feeling? When that happens, we can easily become scared, anxious or sad.

If you feel that way, you can ask the fire to help you turn up your inner fire so that you become more aware of yourself, so that you can feel yourself and know better what you desire in life. When our fire is in balance, it is easier for us to sense what we are passionate about and we simply have more fun," Chief Eaglefeather says, and asks you to think how it feels inside if the inner fire is too weak.

As you sit there looking into the flames you get comfortable.

Maybe you can feel how the fire is nice and warm. Maybe your cheeks warm up and you feel the heat from the fire?

Maybe you see the logs, the flames and the embers?

Maybe you smell the smoke coming from the fire?

Maybe you feel the energy from the fire?

Maybe you hear the crackle from the fire?

"The fire is our friend. If you want, you can borrow the strength of the fire and turn up your own fire," *Chief Eaglefeather* says. "Or maybe turn down your inner fire and make it smaller and calmer, if that feels better to you.

Try to sense how big your inner fire should be for you to be comfortable. The fire helps you to create balance, and gives you a sense of whether you need more or less fire inside."

"See if you can get a sense of the fire inside of yourself and try turning it up and down until it reaches a balance. How will your fire feel at its best inside of you? What does it look like and how does it feel inside of you?" asks *Chief Eaglefeather*.

"A fire has a lot of energy. It can burn for a long time and burn beautifully, if we are careful not to let it go out, or flare up and become too fierce," *Chief Eaglefeather* continues.

"As you have now looked into the fire and felt the heat from it, I am going to tell you another magical quality of this fire. Maybe you see something moving about in the flames?

It looks like someone is dancing inside the fire? Those are the Flamedancers. Let me tell you about them. First, try if you can, to see them as figures, hovering around and dancing in the fire. The Flamedancers are our friends and magical helpers. They are fire energies that live inside the fire. They are very special and have magical powers.

One such magical power is that they can help us cleanse our energy and diffuse excess energy we no longer want to carry with us. They are ready to receive from us the energies we don't want to bring into the first light of tomorrow. We can let go of everything that has built up within us today and that which burdens us, before we go to sleep.

The Flamedancers will receive it, dance with it and help us transform it into peace," Chief Eaglefeather says.

"Some days, there will be a lot to throw onto the fire, other days only very little. It differs. But often we carry excess energy around from negative thoughts, feelings and experiences and we can benefit from throwing this unwanted energy onto the fire and getting rid of it. In this way, we let go of what drags us down and holds us in a lower vibration.

It almost feels like cleaning up inside, so that we can bring in more light, love and joy, and move up into a higher and more joyful and happy vibration."

As you look into the fire you see a beautiful white smoke dancing up in a thin line from the fire. You look at Chief Eaglefeather and ask about the smoke. He smiles to you and replies:

"When the Flamedancers dance in the flames, they transform our darkness into peaceful white smoke, rising from the fire into the sky as a signal of peace, as a signal to the Universe that you are ready to find peace, joy and harmony inside."

"Now, look into the fire and see if you can spot one of the Flamedancers whirling around in there, in a beautiful dance. Look how beautifully they are dancing. Now, if you have excess energy from thoughts, feelings and experiences you found difficult to contain during the day, the Flamedancers are ready to receive all that you feel like throwing onto the fire," Chief Eaglefeather says.

"Maybe someone said something to you that made you sad or angry, or you experienced a feeling you didn't like and you are now ready to let go of the excess energy of this feeling or experience," explains Chief Eaglefeather.

"Maybe you are cross with a friend or someone in your family. Or it could be that you are mad at yourself for something you did, or maybe you are distressed about something you said or didn't say."

"It could also be that you did something which you have regretted, but you still keep beating yourself up about it. All these types of energy from different negative thoughts and experiences you can start throwing onto the fire now."

"Sometimes I make small noises while throwing my thoughts, experiences and the overwhelming energy from my feelings onto the fire, and perhaps I wave my arms towards the fire while doing so," Chief Eaglefeather explains.

"If I am really angry about something, I use my arms to throw all my excess angry energy onto the fire. Then I see how the

Flamedancers whirl around in the flames and receive it from me. And they always peacefully receive all that I throw at them. They take everything we throw into the flames and transform it into a wish of peace and harmony in the most beautiful way," Chief Eaglefeather continues.

"So, throw everything you do not want to carry around onto the fire now; everything that makes you so angry, scared, sad, sorrowful, annoyed or resentful that you feel out of balance. There is no right or wrong way to throw your excess energy onto the fire. It is not the emotions we throw onto the fire, it is the energy that builds up inside of us.

Do it in the way that is just right for you. Take your time to clean up inside of you and throw everything that you do not want to carry into your dreams with you, or into the first light of tomorrow, onto the flames," encourages Chief Eaglefeather.

(Take a longer break. Pause for as long as you can sense that your child is throwing things onto the fire. Sometimes it will be over quickly and at other times it can take longer).

"As you are throwing the overwhelming parts of your feelings, thoughts and experiences onto the fire, perhaps you can start to feel how wonderful it is to get rid of all the things that brought you down. Maybe you feel lighter? Maybe you can sense a light spreading in your body," Chief Eaglefeather says, and continues:

"Maybe you can sense that there is room for more light inside of you when you throw your darker shades of energy onto the fire."

"If there is anything more you want to throw onto the fire, now is the time to do so. Have faith that the Flamedancers will take away everything you are ready to let go of," says Chief Eaglefeather.

♡ ♡ ♡

"Your own inner light is starting to shine stronger and stronger. The more you cleanse, the lighter you become and the brighter you shine. Just like a little sun that comes clear of the clouds. Now, let go of the concerns you had today and start tuning into your light. It's often most easy to see or feel your light around your heart or inside your heart," Chief Eaglefeather says.

"When you are done throwing things onto the fire, just sit and sense the force of the fire and feel the nice warmth coming from the fire," Chief Eaglefeather says.

"And then imagine the size of your inner fire now; do you feel that it is more in balance now? Breathe lovingly into the part of your body where you feel the sensation of inner fire," he says.

"Now that you have cleansed your mind and body of heavy energy, it is time to call in the energies of a higher vibration; we all love to feel this higher vibration. Think about something you really like to do. Something or someone that makes you happy. Really happy!

Think about someone or something that makes you smile, or even better, laugh. And then ask the fire to give you more of that type of passion. It almost feels like you're making a wish.

Think about something you are passionate about, something that lights you up. And ask for more.

And just turn up that feeling. By cleansing your energy of more heavy energy, you have made room for more passion in your body, more love and more light," Chief Eaglefeather explains.

Chief Eaglefeather walks around the fire and hands you all a small wooden stick. He asks you to place it between your hands in front of your hearts. And as you feel your passion in your heart you can let it flow into the stick and fill the stick with your desire for more passion. Take a look at the stick now. Maybe it has changed colour to a colour you love. Maybe your desires have made it change shape.

Now when you are ready you can throw the stick onto the fire. Trust the Flamedancers will know how to dance with your wishes and help you make them come true. The Flamedancers help you enforce the energy of your deepest desires and energies. Watch what happens in the flames as they dance with your desires! Feel what happens in your body. Enjoy the feeling.

Keep filling yourself up with good energy. And know that the Flamedancers are waiting for you to help you cleanse and find more passion. They lift you up to a higher vibration with their dance. All you need to do is use your imagination and trust them.

(Stay here until you sense the child is ready to move on).

Choose an ending

If the child is going to sleep:

Dear_______, now that you have met the Flamedancers, it is time to go to sleep. Remember that you are always welcome back in The Valley of Hearts. I so enjoyed visiting the valley with you today. I can't wait for us to do so again soon. Sweet dreams, sleep tight.

If the child is going on with their day:

Dear_______, now that you have spent beautiful time with the Flamedancers, the time has come to return to this room.

Start by moving your fingers and wiggling your toes up and down.

When you are ready, open your eyes. Remember that you can always come back and visit Chief Eaglefeather whenever you want to.

If you and your child know 'The Children's Meditations In My Heart' *and want to end by filling your hearts with love:*

Before we say goodbye to The Flamedancers' Fire, I would like you to focus your attention on your heart.

Your Love Mountain is quite near. It is a part of the beautiful mountain range of Love Mountains surrounding this amazing valley. Imagine yourself walking to your mountain. Go inside; look at your beautiful heart. See all the colours, feel the warmth, hear the beautiful tunes of love.

Now, find the little 'dial' in your heart and dial it up to fill your beautiful heart with love. It's always nice to fill our hearts with love after we have cleaned up our minds. So just fill up your heart with love and let your love grow and be filled with light, warmth and the most beautiful colours you can imagine.

Just fill up your beautiful heart with love and let the love float around in your beautiful body.

Sweet dreams, my friend, go to sleep with your heart now full of love.

Let's go deeper

Reflections for parents after the meditation

I hope both you and your child have enjoyed the meditation. In this chapter I will go a little deeper into the characteristics of the fire element. At the end of the book you will find a Notes section if you or your child feel like writing more of your observations or reflections down.

Both before and after meditation with a child, I always recommend that we, as caregivers, take a little time to pay attention to our inner wellbeing as well. Do you also need to balance your inner fire?

Would it create more balance for you if you could turn down your own fire a bit? Or do you feel a need for more fire? You can go back to the questions I asked in the introduction about your inner fire, if you want to explore your inner fire in greater depth.

Walk the talk

Also sense whether you yourself could benefit from throwing excess energy built up from your thoughts, emotions, feelings or experiences from your own day or life onto the fire.

I often join my kids when they visit the fire and clear my own energy at the same time. You might find it easier in the beginning to first help your child and then do your own meditation afterwards.

This exercise can be so liberating and is such a good support for adults too. By learning to tend to our own inner fire, we automatically become lifelong teachers for our children as they mirror our behaviour.

If you breathe deep into your stomach instead of getting cross, your child will notice a change in your behaviour. Also, if you have been shining too dimly for some time, it will affect your children positively, when you begin to turn up your light.

Every time we, as parents, develop and change our behaviour we must allow children a little time to get used to the new energy. Have patience.

Time to dig a little deeper

Perhaps it will be of benefit for you as a parent to reflect on what typically weighs on your child at night time. Think about what feelings or experiences your child might want to rid themselves of before they sleep. Maybe talk with them about it and steer them in the right direction.

As parents, it is important that we receive and harbour our children's feelings and encourage them to get to know and become confident with all of their feelings. It often helps parents I work with to think of their children as little scientists working in an emotional lab. They study different feelings they may be experiencing and mix them up to test different outcomes. Sometimes they have to study an emotion longer than we like as parents. Be patient with it. If you have young children you probably recognize this exploration from different ways of role playing. If they play family they often take on the same role in the imaginary family several times until it is time to experiment with another role.

We need all emotions

It is important for me to state that the purpose of this meditation isn't to remove feelings that are perceived as wrong, dark or negative. That wouldn't be good for us. We need all of our emotions. Think about it: what would happen if we didn't have darker emotions to contrast our light? You necessarily need one to have the other. There are benefits to all our emotions.

There is a good chance that some of the darker feelings are shameful for you. And there is a good chance that you are passing some of your childhood emotions on to your child. If you carry some unsettled emotional patterns around from your own childhood, there is a good chance you react more strongly when you see these emotions in your child. I strongly recommend mirror work for parents to enable you to become aware of your trigger reactions, as it's likely your children will bring these to light. If we use provocations from our children to grow and heal our own wounds, we can prevent so much of our own 'stuff' from being passed on to the next generation. I strongly believe that many of the problems we see in our children have much more to do with their environment and us than with them as a child.

So, if not emotions what are we throwing onto the fire? To me it feels like it's the excess energy that can build so easily within us, that becomes stuck inside of us and even manifests as physical tension. It's time to let go of this stuck, negative energy that's weighing us down. It's energy that is no longer of service to us. So, we cleanse with fire.

Fire in balance

All children benefit from this exercise, also the ones whose inner fire is already balanced. Children who have a balanced fire element are characterised by knowing what they want. They are passionate, full of energy, brave, have a joy for life, are optimistic, loving, show their love, have an appetite for life, are charismatic - all the while being able to set boundaries in a good way.

Uncontrolled fire

Having a lot of fire inside as a child (and adult) can be quite a challenge. These children are often characterised by their fierce temper, large fluctuations in temperament, outbursts, a lot of anger, impatience, hyperactivity, and they show a tendency to exaggerate.

Some of these children lose their temper, scream, shout, stamp their feet, throw things through the air, bite, hit or kick. When the inner fire is out of control it often engulfs and overwhelms the child.

At a certain stage of rage the child can seem unreachable. The picture that comes to my mind is of a raging volcano. Some children become all red-faced when they lose their temper, and find it difficult to control their eruptions. Sometimes they even erupt out of the blue. This feeling is not pleasant for the child, the parents or the surroundings. The older the child gets the more embarrassing these outbursts become.

When a child is very upset it affects parents, classmates, friends and other people who spend time with the child. As adults around a high-tempered child it is important we remain calm and practice our breathing.

Don't join their drama

Try to remember that the child is hurting and crying out for help, even though the words they are using may not sound like a cry for help.

Here is a method I have found that works with high-tempered kids:

1. Stay calm and lend your child your peace

The first and maybe most important thing when your child throws a tantrum, is for you to stay calm. Don't join their drama! Think of it like this: if you stay calm you open up a space in your energy for your child to crawl into and find peace and calmness. Lend your child your peace.

And just for this exercise, visualize the space you lend to your child if you lose your temper too.

For smaller outbursts it might be enough that you just sit calmly and breathe deeply next to your child. If you need more tools than just your breathing you can try to recognise the anger for what it is by saying: "I can see/feel that you are very angry/sad/upset." When the child senses that you have understood their message, you have created a connection. Now you can try to comfort them.

When the child feels understood and that you have 'met' them where they are emotionally, the worst of their anger often dissipates. The child can then hear what you are saying and learn from your teachings.

2. Refuel and share the energy of the Universe

I have also experimented with consciously sharing an energy stream with my child. What I do is imagine pulling down a stream of energy from the Universe. I see this golden white light coming down through my crown chakra (top of my head) and let it flow to my heart. I then open my heart and direct the light to my child. As a parent of young kids (and sometimes older as well) we only have so much energy in our bodies. The Universe however is abundant in energy and light, and by becoming conscious of how you attract this energy you can access it and share it with your child. I love this way of parenting and it helped me immensely when I was a mother of two young children. As it runs through your heart it will feel familiar to your child, but you won't lose your energy. As it runs through you it also recharges your own battery at the same time.

3. See beyond the situation and translate

When your child has calmed down, you can try to see beyond the anger and explore what caused the outburst in the first place. To see beyond the current situation, we use our intuition or third eye chakra in our foreheads. We can close our eyes and look up towards the intersection of our eyebrows to see much deeper. This will train your intuition. If this is new to you, you can also try to analyse the situation from a more practical viewpoint. What could be an obvious reason? Very often you will find simple answers to your child's frustrations.

There is a good chance your child is:
- tired
- overstimulated
- hungry
- or any combination of the above!

As a parent we get a lot of help by zooming out and taking a broader view of any given situation. Often our child hasn't slept enough; they have had too much going on or they are "hangry" (hungry + angry = hangry). Next step is then to provide what is needed. Help the child take a nap, get to bed earlier, feed them or clear the schedule if too much is going on.

4. Cleanse

After such drama other feelings will often follow, for instance feelings of inadequacy, guilt or shame. It is important that we can also acknowledge these feelings in our children.

When we have recognised these feelings for what they are and have listened to our children, the fire meditations can be a way of helping them to clear their mind and move on. When we give children, who are very much influenced by their feelings, a tool to clean out the bad experiences and thoughts they create by virtue of their own behaviour, we also give them an opportunity to reflect upon the outcomes of their feelings in a safe space. More importantly, we give them a chance to clear their minds and start afresh.

High-tempered parents

As parents, it is also unpleasant when our own inner volcano starts boiling or erupting. To shout at our children makes us feel so uncomfortable. It also provokes feelings of being a lousy parent, not good enough, or not being able to handle them. Feelings such as inadequacy, guilt, shame and remorse can fester inside of you.

If this resonates with you, I recommend you face the feelings head on, explore them, recognise them, and learn from them. You too can throw excess energy onto the fire so that you do not wake up the following day still carrying the heavy energy these feelings often bear. We can learn a lot from our mistakes and at the same time move on to a better starting point for the new day.

I often see parents getting upset when their children lose their temper in public. And I imagine that the same scenery plays out at home - maybe there is even more fury as nobody is watching. As parents we have a choice to keep calm. Just breathe for a second and survey the situation before you give in to your own behavioural triggers. Understanding that we don't need to join the drama of a tempered child is the way forward for us as parents. Understanding this is such a relief. Nothing good ever came out of two raging fires feeding on each other. In fact, such reactive rage and fire has caused much sadness throughout our history.

As parents we are given the chance to be the role models we may not have had when we were children. If you have a lot of temper, take a moment to think about how your inner fire was handled when you were a child, and how your parents reacted to you when your fire erupted. If your parents reacted with fury fire to your fire, there is a good chance you are mirroring their reactions to your child's fire. That is all you've known how to be. But you can choose to change that.

Also, be aware of how your work, friends, family might upset you and how it so easily affects your way of parenting.

Five steps to peaceful parenting

By using these simple five steps you can learn to keep calm and parent more peacefully:

1. Focus on your breath – breathe deeper
2. Pause – clear your mind
3. Survey the situation - see beyond the situation
4. Become conscious – understand your role as a role model
5. Parent peacefully – help your child.

Your role as a parent is to guide your child and help steer your child through the storm safely. You are the light house! By applying the five steps above, you also teach your child to use the same calming techniques, equipping your little volcano with the tools they need to avoid full eruption mode. It is a double win for both of you and many beautiful things can grow from here between you. As a parent, learning to stay calm and stay out of your child's drama provides such a relief.

Once I was teaching in Manchester, England, and a taxi driver asked me about my work. I told him about conscious parenting and parenting from the heart. He reflected for a moment and asked, "But how do you discipline with love?" I told him I don't believe in disciplining children. He then asked, "But how will they ever listen to you?" My heart sank and I replied that respect is something we earn out of the respect we show our children, by leading them and helping them in a peaceful manner and by being good role models. Respect forced out of fear is not healthy and will only create more turbulence and push your child away.

As a kid I had a lot of temper myself, and as an Aries, fire is one of my key elements. When my children were young I wasn't familiar with the meditation tools I now advocate so passionately in my books. I didn't like who I became when I got upset with them and yelled at them. So, I found new and better ways to deal with my own temper. And staying calm as a mother, has helped me to raise my girls in a peaceful way. For many years now, I have not had to raise my voice to my girls, and the respect that grows out of this loving way of parenting is so much more powerful than any respect grown out of fear.

Too little fire

The fire meditation is also good for children with too little fire, who maybe find it difficult to gain a sense of Self, make choices or set boundaries. They can easily feel overlooked, indifferent, distanced, joyless, without spark, without enthusiasm, or even worse: extinguished and sad.

If we don't really know what we want and don't shine a light on ourselves, others tend to overlook us and our feelings; we yield our power and allow others to steer our course, which can feel unpleasant for children and adults alike.

For children with little fire, insight into the fire element and a reminder of its force will feed more fire into their system.

We often call these children "the invisible children". Something or someone in their upbringing has made them believe it is better if they don't show emotion, if they stay shallow. They have been taught that it is safer to stay within the shadows and to not make a fuss.

However, the more dimmed their inner fire becomes, the harder it is for the child to navigate. Without our fire, we can't feel our passion and it becomes very hard to make decisions and choose a path. These children are often indifferent. They allow their siblings or friends to decide which games to play. They pick the same flavour of ice cream as their best friend. They never stand first in line. They observe the behaviour of others and are masters of camouflage and mirroring their surroundings. Their needs are often overlooked by parents, teachers and other caregivers. They can come across as shy.

When passion is hard to find inside a child's heart, doubt can easily take over and these children may begin to question their own behaviour and even their place in the world. When doubt takes over, fear often sets in, and if we don't, as parents, pay attention, the road to anxiety is paved.

If you meditate with a child with little fire, I recommend putting more effort into the first part of the meditation, where the child is sitting by the fire and is prompted to turn up their inner fire.

It can be a good idea to proceed slowly in this case, as fire can be intimidating to some of these children.

Reflect upon your own fire as well. Maybe it is time for you to visit your fire and turn up that passion a notch in your own life.

Dimmed parents

If you feel your inner fire is dimmed as a parent, it is time to tend to your own fire too. In my coaching I often see parents who have let society's social norms dim their lights and many, quite unwittingly, pass this 'acceptance' on to their children. In fact, they often come to see me because they see some of their own miseries repeating in their children.

These parents have often had a hard time living with their own dimmed light and they get really frightened when they see this lack of light mirrored in their child. To be honest I wish they had come for coaching much sooner. I wish they had had the same love for themselves that they show their children. Too many parents have found a way of living with a dimmed light and don't fully understand the consequences until they see their own hardships mirrored in their child's experiences. However, it is never too late! And when our children become our teachers in this magical way, they show us that change is possible, even though they maybe can't verbalize it.

I recommend that you express your gratitude to your child for being your teacher and for helping you to grow.

If your child is strong-willed and your light is dim, it is also important to tend to your fire. Maybe your child is trying to teach you about the fire element and how to find balance. It wouldn't surprise me. Our children come with such great teachings. The meditation in this book will help your child understand about their inner fire and to turn it up (or down). And of course, there are also lessons to be learned if you are high-tempered and your child is more dimmed.

Let nature help you

One of my ambitions with this book is also to encourage you to learn from nature and spend more time in nature. When was the last time you looked into the flames of a real fire? I love making bonfires in my garden and connecting to fire. Build a fire, get your sticks and roast marshmallows, bake pancakes or make popcorn over the fire.

It is also possible to connect to the fire element by lighting a candle or other simple things that involve fire in our everyday routines. Remember to always be with your children around fire and to make it a safe environment for them.

Teach your child to honour the fire. Give thanks when you light the fire in a respectful manner. Maybe say a little prayer: Thank you for the fire that is keeping me warm and teaching me to light my fire/ tend to my fire.

Or an affirmation: The fire in me honours the fire in you. We light each other up.

Bring in perspective

Also, talk to your children about the fire at the centre of the earth, the ball of fire that is the sun, tell them how there is or at least was, fire in all of the stars or study the volcanoes. You can also talk about which animals contain a lot of fire, such as dragons, lions or fireflies. Maybe you are into astrology and will have fun looking up your zodiac sign. The fire signs are Aries, Leo, and Sagittarius. You can talk about places where you experience or use fire in your daily lives, such as when cooking. You can also talk about the different forms of fire energy - like solar energy. Find fire in your daily lives and remind your child of the different types and manifestations of fire.

Another tip is to wear the colours of fire in your clothes as you explore the element.

You can also study the element of fire by tuning into your solar plexus chakra and learning more about this third chakra which represents our inner fire.

Lift the vibration

The last part of the meditation is also important. That is when we load passion into our system. As we have let go of excess energy and thrown it on the fire, there is room to attract the new energy of a higher vibration.

I invite you to play with passion in your everyday household as well. Ask your children about their passions. Applaud them for being passionate. Show interest in what excites them.

Ask questions such as: what are you passionate about right now? What was the most exciting thing that happened at school today? Or how can you make tomorrow even more exciting?

If your child has too little fire and doesn't show much passion begin by the small things and small questions and have them feel into their desire - strawberry or kiwi fruit? And then gradually delve deeper and deeper about their passions.

Also talk about your own passion and show your passion to your children, partners, family and friends. Smile to the shop assistant, pick up the parcel for a neighbour, get excited about your friend's passion, make your favourite meal and express your joy even more than you usually do. Turn up the fire, cherish it and let it guide you to a passionate life.

Thank you for meditating with us and teaching these important techniques to your child.

The fire in me
sees the fire in you
and salutes it.
Thank you for
tending to your fire.

Let's light up
our children and
empower them to
fall in love with life
and shine even brighter.

Children are born
as light and love.
Let's remind them
and help them
stay connected.

#together

Notes on your experiences

We learned a lot when we
made this book for you
- we hope you did too!

About the author

The book series The Valley of Hearts is written by Gitte Winter Graugaard (b. 1977), who is also the author of the bestseller *The Children's Meditations in my Heart* and several other books.

Gitte is passionate about writing books to strengthen imagination in children, as well as nurture their intuition and create balance in life.

Gitte holds a Masters Degree in Business Administration and has worked in Communication, specialising in storytelling. She is also a trained Life Mastery Coach, Heartcore Mentor, Mindfulness Instructor and Conscious Transformer. Today she mainly shares her knowledge through intuitive storytelling and meditation.

However, the most important knowledge, namely to listen to yourself and live your dreams, originates in Gitte's own life, which is, and always has been, filled with love and choices of the heart.

www.gittewintergraugaard.dk

About the illustrator

Very often meditation opens up avenues for creativity. Elsie Ralston has illustrated these books. She was born and raised in Peru. Love for her husband brought her to Denmark. Below you can see a picture from the process of producing the illustrations for this book.

You can find Elsie on: www.elsieralston.com

Do you like to draw
with colours?

Now it's your turn - be creative

You can benefit from drawing the fire and all the things that are going onto it. On the next page your child can also colour *The Flame-dancers' Fire*. Help your child to get to know their feelings and to become comfortable with them by being creative.

Take notes

In the days after the fire meditation, I recommend that you talk to your child about what the child threw onto the fire, if they want to talk about it. In the following pages you can take notes. These notes can become very valuable for your child in the future when they might need to reconnect to their fire element again as adults. You can encourage an older child to use the next pages as a diary about their experiences with the meditations.

What did you throw on to the fire?

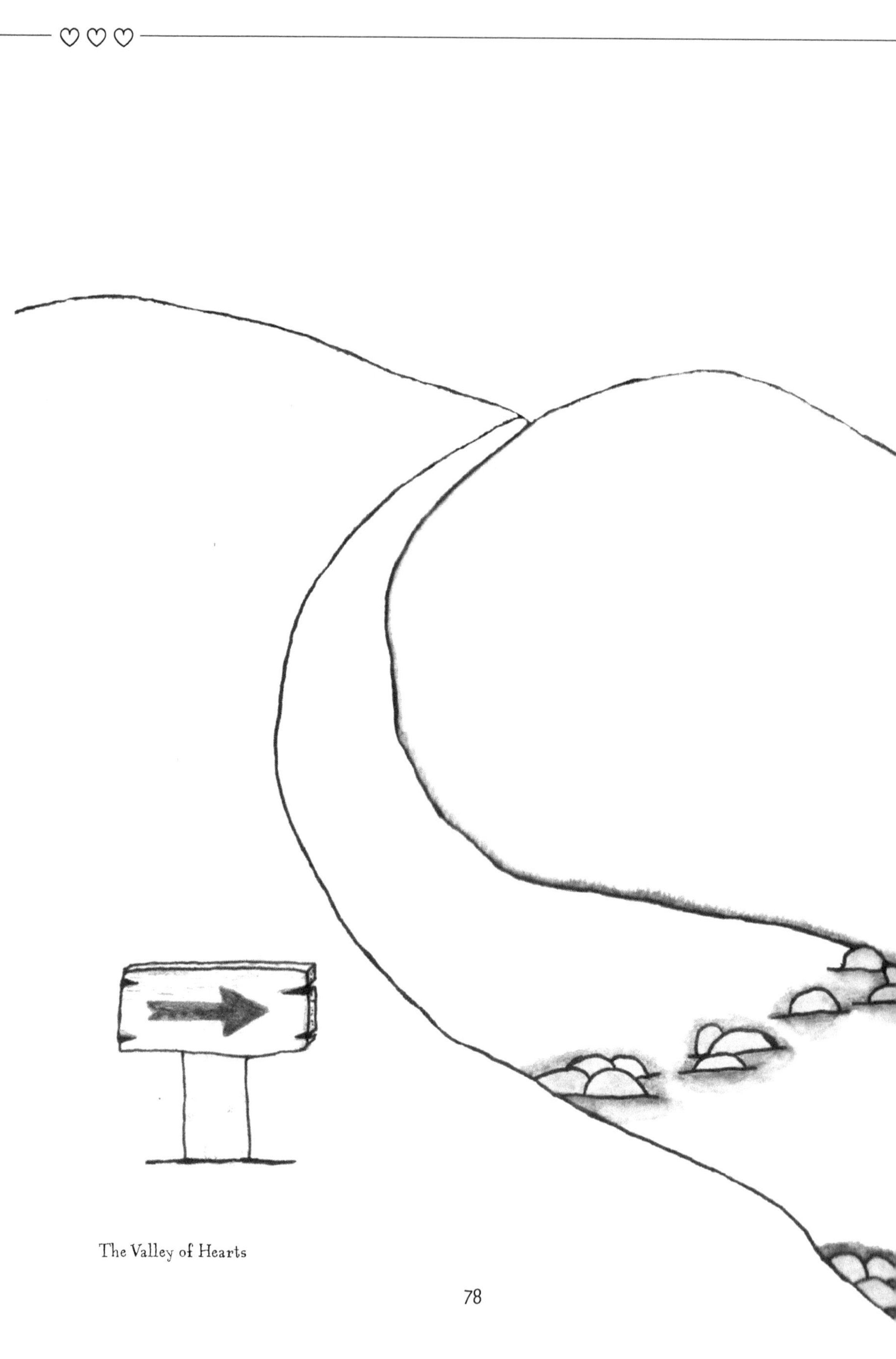

The Valley of Hearts

Chief Eaglefeather from
The Valley of Hearts

What do you think he is looking at? You can draw it if you like.

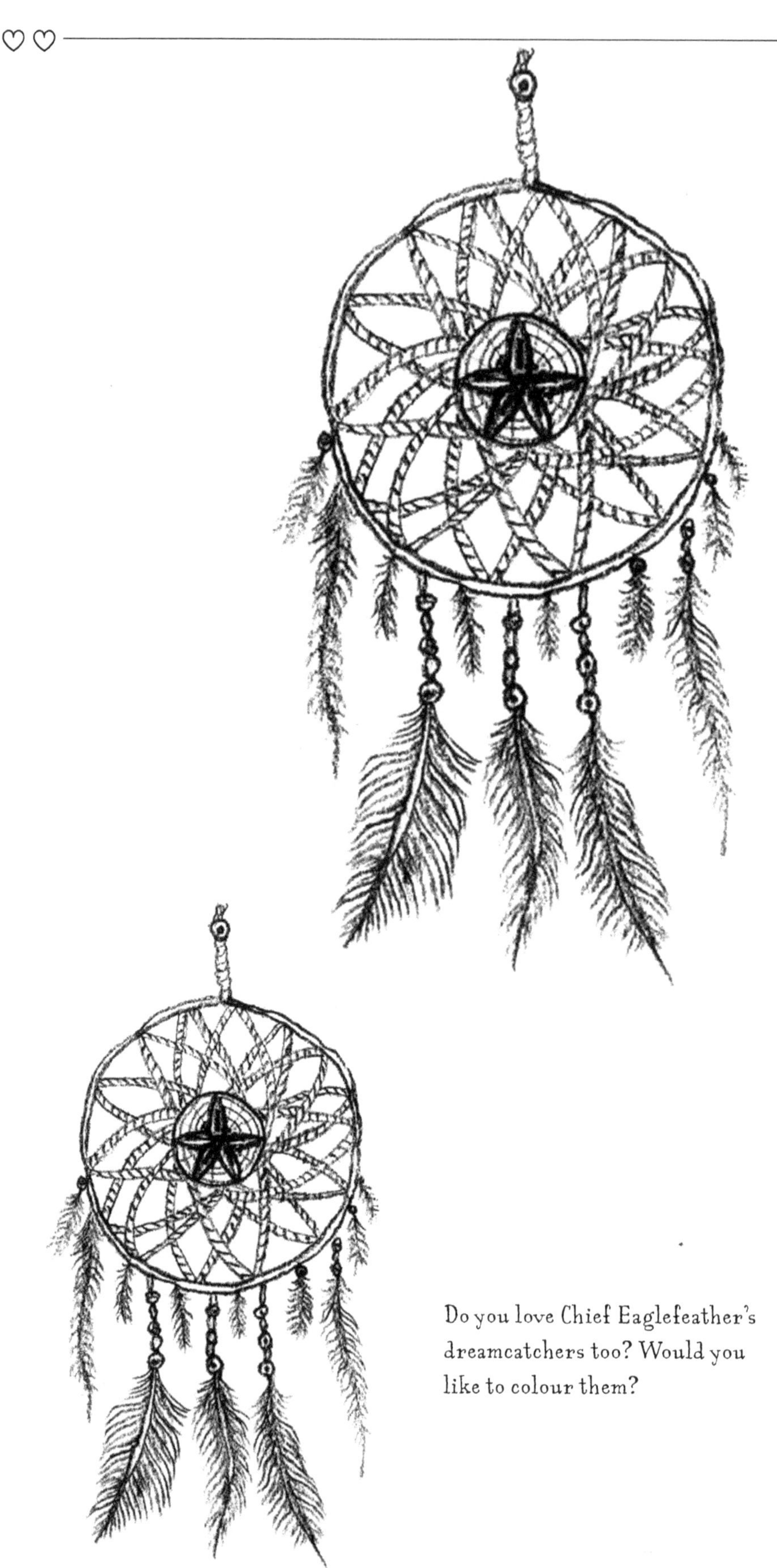

Do you love Chief Eaglefeather's dreamcatchers too? Would you like to colour them?

Design your own dreamcatcher

The Clear Cascade

The Deep Meadow

The Mild Winds

Did you like the
meditation and
would you like more?

Meet Chief Eaglefeather
Meditations for children
BEDTIME STORIES
Let sleep come easily with these meditations.
Create a deep connection with your child and help them to recharge.
No1
Gitte Winter Graugaard
The Flamedancers' Fire
Meditations for children
BEDTIME STORIES
Let sleep come easily with this FIRE meditation.
Create a deep connection with your child and help them to recharge.
No2
The Clear Cascade
Meditations for children
BEDTIME STORIES
Let sleep come easily with this WATER meditation.
Create a deep connection with your child and help them to recharge.
The Deep Meadow
Meditations for children
BEDTIME STORIES
Let sleep come easily with this EARTH meditation.
Create a deep connection with your child and help them to recharge.
No4
Gitte Winter Graugaard
The Mild Winds
Meditations for children
BEDTIME STORIES
Let sleep come easily with this AIR meditation.
Create a deep connection with your child and help them to recharge.
No5
Gitte Winter Graugaard

All the books in the series The Valley of Hearts

In the first book, "Meet Chief Eaglefeather" I gave you two meditations.

As your child becomes more comfortable you can move further into the valley to encounter each of the elements. As you reach each new stage of the journey, new books and more meditations will be waiting for you.

"The Flamedancers' Fire" is book number two. You can benefit from using this meditation for children with lots of temper and conversely, for children with too little fire inside. Getting to know how to turn down or up your inner fire is crucial for how you cope in life.

"The Clear Cascade" in book number three is such a blessing to sensitive children and children prone to worry. It teaches us to cleanse our energy from other people before sleeping, which makes it a lot easier to feel our own energy and our own needs and boundaries.

Book number four is "The Deep Meadow", it is beneficial for all children in the Digital Age. Most children today need help to ground themselves.

We get to fly with "The Mild Winds" in book number five. The little daydreamers will love this meditation. However, it can also help children who need more perspective and creativity.

Each element has its own magical quality, which can be used to achieve peace of mind and to create better balance inside.

Please visit: www.thevalleyofhearts.com

The Children's Meditations

IN MY HEART

This bestselling book is teaching thousands of children to find their Love Mountain and fill themselves with love. It works very well with "Heartlight". You get four amazing meditations in one book. They also help your child to sleep and teaches your child about empathy, appreciation, connection and so much more. Now selling in more than 20 countries in multiple languages.

www.inmyheart.eu

HEARTLIGHT

Teach your child to shine

This little book is an obvious sequel to "In My Heart", as the fifth meditation. Here, your child learns to turn up their inner light in the mountain of love and carry it around the whole body to spread their inner light. This meditation is also part of the book "The Monster Manual for children who worry a lot". Find out how to make your child a light bearer.

www.heartlight.eu

A Global Mission

Gitte Winter Graugaard is on a mission to help ONE MILLION CHILDREN and their families thrive through bedtime meditation. She is an expert in peaceful bedtime routines. She is a bestselling and award-winning author, and a TEDx speaker.

Her books are helping thousands of children to sleep in more than 20 countries. Gitte always reminds us to parent ourselves first before we parent our children and become aware of what we radiate.

To find more inspiration to conscious parenting and better sleep, you can follow Gitte's blog on:

www.gittewintergraugaard.dk

To book Gitte for speaking or workshops go to:

www.gittewintergraugaard.com

Gitte talking at TEDx Peterborough UK, April 2019

Gitte is on a mission
to teach 1 MILLION children
to meditate. You can help her
by sharing this book and your
experiences with others. Ask for
her books at your local library,
or at your favorite bookshop and
use as presents to those you love.
Support her mission.

See you next time ...

Thank you
for teaching
your child
to meditate.

www.ingramcontent.com/pod-product-compliance
Ingram Content Group UK Ltd.
Pitfield, Milton Keynes, MK11 3LW, UK
UKHW061953290726
14090UKWH00021B/1206